Systemology

The "How To Guide" for How To Turbocharge your business systematically

Clive I. Jones

Systemology

Disclaimer
For clarity and conciseness here are the two most important legalities regarding this book in plain English.
1. The reader assumes all responsibility of this publication for the use of these materials and information.
2. This book is not intended as legal or financial advice.

ISBN 13: 978-1481085878
First Edition

Published by:
Jonesci Pty Ltd,
PO Box 8046, Summerland Point, NSW 2259
www.jonesci.com
www.clivejones.com.au

Dedicated to all who have helped me to the experience I have shared here.

About the Author:

Clive I. Jones.

34 years Business Management Experience including:
- 3 x Management troubleshooting jobs
- 4 year Business Apprenticeship
- Family of Small Business Owners...Father, Mother, Uncles, Father In Law,
- 4 years systemising Fathers Business
- 19 years in own businesses (4 different ones)
- 7 years as software implementer/trainer
- 5 years Business Consultant
- 8+ years as Business & Executive Coach...continuing.

Foreword by Brad Sugars

The backbone of a successful long term business, is not just sales and marketing, it's the ability to implement and follow systems... Problem is, this is one of the most misunderstood areas of business, which is strange as it's something that's quite simple to implement.

In my Business Coaching business ActionCOACH my team of Coaches all teach our clients how to build a *"Commercial, Profitable, Enterprise That Works, Without You"*. For that to happen you need to leverage yourself out of the daily operations, but how can you ensure that things run as well when you are not there.

As one of our longer standing Coaches, I know Clive would teach you that this covers all areas of business, from the foundations of basic business in time management, financial management, planning and delivery of your product or service, through everything to do with Sales and Marketing, and building a winning Team.

If you are serious about building your business to give you the results and freedom or choices that you desire for the long term, then you can't do it all yourself, you need a team that can do it for you. After all, none of us set out in business to build ourselves a job... we are looking to multiply our efforts and build an asset for when we are ready to sell.

In writing this book I have found that Clive has taken what is not the most exciting topic and made it interesting, concise and easy to follow, providing you with a simple "system" to follow for implementing systems in your business. His depth of experience shows through and he keeps the content simple and easy to follow... just as the systems that you develop should be if you follow this process.

You'll use LOGIC and PROFIT here to get you a process that will help you build and refine your business systems to a high standard. In my series of books a lot of what I have written about is systems to follow to achieve the best outcomes... this book helps you to build these into your business so that your team can use these tools effectively, and as I said, consistently.

This book is laid out as a system in itself, so I recommend that you follow the steps, and start working on developing your systems to build yourself a Commercial Profitable Enterprise, that CAN work without you... then you'll have a real asset to give you that freedom of choice that so many are looking for.

Brad Sugars – Founder & CEO ActionCOACH
Brad Sugars has established a worldwide success of many thousands of businesses through his team of Business Coaches, winning many accolades along the way. An author of many business growth books too his vision is "World Abundance Through Business Re-education".

"If there is anything you do without documenting it, you'll continue having to do it yourself until you do"

Brad Sugars

Contents

Introduction

There has to be a system, right? A set of rules to follow or processes to implement that successful business owners use. Where is the manual... the book that tells you how to do all that?

I have read many books and learned from a lot of people... a whole atlas full of roadmaps to achieve a wide range of different things that we all need to learn in business, and realise that to many, it is simply a case of so much to do and so little time.... so where do I start?

This book is my attempt to help you through this in a logical process... a system to follow if you like. After all, slavery is supposed to be dead, isn't it... but many times I can talk to a business owner and when they work out their income divided across the number of hours they work and relate it to that of many junior workers it is a sad reality that many are receiving far less. For most, they have poor or no systems in place to make the business run efficiently in the first place so are often at the ransom of expensive employees helping them to hold things together. With systems in place we have less reliance on employee intelligence and can have more accountability to ensure tasks are completed properly.

I'm a mad keen yacht racer and a Yacht-Master Instructor for well over 20 years, and I can't help running the comparison of how we have countless systems and processes to follow in that sport to be able to reach the top.

From simple checklists to make sure we have all the safety gear on board, and briefing all crew members where it's hidden... through to the obvious... plotting the race or voyage so we know where we are headed. Imagine that.. just wandering down the dock, casting off and setting sail... without having any kind of a plan or system to follow.

Even for that initial activity there is a need for a process or system to follow... we need to check a few things before starting the motor, then, when it's on do we have cooling water running through it...check...

OK, so is everyone in position, which way is the wind and current going to push the boat when we cast off, so which ropes are not needed and can be let go first, and which ones do we use to make sure we keep the boat under control.

We haven't left the dock yet and the process goes on... yet an average team following a simple system can make it look blissfully easy.

I come from a family of small business owners, manufacturers, engineers, and service professionals and my background from leaving school has been in business management.... theory and practical experience combined.

I've run my own businesses since 1993 and prior to that had a knack of making my jobs run independently of me.

Let's think about that for a moment... how would it be for you to make yourself redundant in your own business....so that it actually runs well when you are not there. That's not to say you can't go and play in it... but you do then have the choices. Or you might be a department manager like I was, and want to enjoy your work, and have the opportunity to work more strategically, running the best department rather than constantly fighting fires and going home stressed every day. Managers roles are to ensure their teams follow appropriate systems, and to step up when the system is inadequate, such as when exceptions to the rule crop up.

I once had a job managing Inventory and Freight, which was in a mess when I started. After a short while the MD realised I had that all under control so he gave my bosses job to me, running Purchasing and Production as well...promotion!! I therefore had to set about systemising those roles too and before long I was knocking off again at 4pm with everything done and all going smoothly.... no stress, no unpaid work, and a great social life because I could get out of work on time and relax knowing everything was under control.

Enjoying a challenge I jumped straight into another job where they had a major stock control issue. $12M worth of computer hardware and software... all the popular stuff.... and only 48% accuracy in the computer... a disaster waiting to happen. A simple systematic approach to identifying errors, mainly procedural, and putting systems or procedures in place, from Sales, through to Accounts, Purchasing, Goods in, Despatch, Returns, Management... the list goes on, we lifted the accuracy to 99.8% at the following stock-take. I tend to get bored when things have started working for me, so decided I needed a bigger challenge and started working for myself.

Now a Business Coach, I spend most of my time helping business owners just like you implement systems to their businesses, with the aim of giving them the freedom to choose whether they work or not.

One of my favourite words is "Leverage", and I'm constantly thinking, how can we use the power of leverage to benefit this business or situation.

Just like putting a crowbar under something to give you more power to move something, or a set of pulley blocks to decrease the amount of energy or effort you need to apply when pulling the rope, I like to explore and create systems and processes that once you've established them, your work is done, and you can get your team to do it... consistently over and over again.

So why do systems make things so much easier...?
A dictionary definition of systems is.... *"a complex whole, a set of connected things or parts, an organized body of things"*.

It's all about creating a series of events or a structure to ensure that there is consistency, efficiency and predictability with a higher level of reliability and speed. It sets a standard for "Best Practice" in productivity and reduced dependency on you with an easier reference point for initial and on-going training. In a nutshell, they can lead to you enjoying more time off!!

Sounds good doesn't it... but why isn't there a whole bunch of systems already written down to help me make life easy... I guess at the end of the day there are so many different things that everyone does, and so many variations of each it would be a tall order to produce such a beast.

My goal in producing this book is to give you a series of useful ideas to help you implement your own systems in the most efficient way. In doing so, I will share with you many of my experiences over the last 30+ years in business management, along with credit due to those places where I can remember picking up those that I didn't think of myself. In other words, I'm not about to re-invent the wheel when there are many masters that I can point you towards for particular aspects for further reference.

So where should we start to implement systems in our business... think of things that need to be done correctly every single time.

Any repetitive, routine work or where critical steps are completed. If you can focus on the Routine any exceptions can be managed by your team as you'll have sets of rules and options to guide them to make appropriate decisions and possibly implement additional systems to handle these variances.

Just remember... If there is anything you do without documenting it, you'll continue having to do it yourself until you do...

Now... it has been said that to have rigid systems in place will stifle creativity and lateral thinking in an organisation. Be aware that this can have an element of truth about it if you want it to happen, however, following the two models in this book and encouraging or rewarding innovation for improving existing systems would actually reverse that potential...

It will also encourage more creativity as your team will be starting from a position of strength in having "a" system to follow rather than the state of confusion that surrounds having nothing in place.

But what if I am a one man band?

Now, you'll note that my language in this book refers on the whole to working with your team, and developing systems for your team to use. So it's important for me to highlight here and now, that everything can apply to the "soloprenuer", those who work on their own, either in a business, or in a job.

 The efficiency benefits still apply, and it makes it easier to get others to help out when you need it or are ready to branch out. The less the business is reliant upon the space between your ears having to remember everything, the more likely it is going to be able to thrive.

Also, if and when you decide to move on, up or out, it becomes a much more valuable asset to sell as the systems are already prepared and it is much easier for someone else to take over.

Action Steps:

Take a moment now to write in here 7 key tasks repeated frequently in your business that are not written down.

1. •

2. •

3. •

4. •

5. •

6. •

7. •

"Insanity is doing the same thing over and over again, expecting different results".

Chapter 1

Why do I need systems..?

This is the "show me the money chapter"... why would you go to the effort of creating systems in your business.

Systemology is about turbo-charging your business – to work without you - systematically..., in other words... how to make yourself redundant from routine tasks enabling you the choice to either enjoy the rewards of a business that runs well while you are not there, or to work more on strategic and other special projects of interest to you..

Are you looking to make it easier to run your business? Do you want to take control and make it less reliant on you being there all the time?
You might be looking to reproduce what you are doing well, and franchise or set up additional operations elsewhere.
You might be looking to capitalise on the value of the business when you sell it as part of your retirement plan.
Maybe you're thinking that you just can't find the right staff as no-one ever does it like you?

Let's explore some areas that your business or life that might be adversely affected right now, which could all be better handled by implementing some good systems into your business.

 As you read through this list consider how each of these items or problems could be costing you in both Time and Money...and in business, time is money so *maybe even write it down in the margin to come back to later...*

Financial Issues...
- Lack of Cash flow management
- Stock mis-management
- Minimal or poor tracking of costs and margins
- Waste not being measured
- Doing extras without charging clients – giving away your time
- Not estimating quantities correctly and having to do last minute purchases from the local store
- Purchasing small, uneconomical quantities
- Not knowing if Hiring or Buying would be cheaper
- Using estimates or guesses and not recording Actual work time
- Accepting variation requests without costing them first and documenting

Operations / Quality Issues
- Re-doing incorrectly completed tasks
- No defined outcomes or targets
- Lack of consistency or routine

- Having to correct minor defects that slip through
- Not checking quality at completion of each stage of production
- Not clarifying your expectation of job quality then having to re-do it.
- Constantly putting out spot fires

Exit or Expansion Strategies...
- No chance of taking regular holidays trusting the business will continue to run successfully.
- No succession plan to replace yourself with the right people to run it for you.
- How to expand to multiple outlets or territories.
- Need to create a franchise system that creates profitable franchisees
- Missing opportunities to take the company international.

Sales Opportunities...
- Not knowing what uniquely sets my business head and shoulders above the competition.
- Poor sales conversion.
- How to get clients to come back again.
- Getting bigger sales from clients when they are buying.
- Lack of, or in-consistent Opportunity follow-ups
- Quotes that go nowhere

Marketing Processes...
- Lack of persuasive, reliable and inexpensive ways to generate more leads or prospects...

- No step by step marketing plan to significantly increase new business, consistently.
- Spending on Marketing without Measuring return.

Communication
- Going to client visits only to find the key people were not there
- Poor communication of delays or changes in project timing
- Not confirming everyones clear understanding when giving out instructions (then things go pear-shaped)
- Taking unnecessary phones calls from your team because they have nowhere else to refer to.

Management
- Having a system for controlling, managing and reporting the company finances.
- Lack of an organizational chart and position descriptions.
- Procrastination through lack of a decision making process
- Sick of talk fests and anxious to start activity

Team Management Systems...
- Micro-Management of Others
- Poor Delegation / Insufficient Guidance or support
- Understand process of how to lead rather than simply manage
- Ad-hoc recruiting not attracting the right team.
- Lack of an ongoing training program to get the team to be more effective and more productive.

- Not trained to deliver superior levels of customer service efficiently.
- Poor use of time and working reactively, putting out fires.

Planning / Preparation Systems...
- Creating documents from scratch without using templates
- Scheduling or re-scheduling people and/ or tasks
- Unnecessary out of hours work / overtime
- Waiting for others to complete their tasks
- No clear or powerful personal or business goals detailed
- Lack of a clear vision for my company for everyone to aim for.
- No action plan to keep us focused on what really is important.

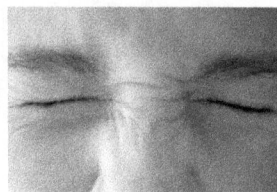 **Each one of these challenges or frustrations are born from a lack of good systems. Inconsistency and mistakes come from flying blind and merely "hoping" that your team will do it the right way every time.**

Action Steps:
Take a moment now to write in here the main reasons for developing *your* systems in *your* business.

1. ●

2. ●

3. ●

4. ●

5. ●

What are the reasons listed above costing you in lost opportunity each year?

● Total _____

Chapter 2.

Systemology

Turbo-charging your business.... systematically

Consider this...

.... It's 9am tomorrow morning and the phone rings... it is one of your key employees with some bad news... for you, at least. They have just been notified of an inheritance and won't be in today... or tomorrow, in fact never again. It's about now that you realise there are a whole stack of things that need to be done, and they have all the information in their heads... no-one else knows how to do the job, and nothing is written down anywhere for someone to try to pick up and run with.

Now there are a number of similar stories with a potentially similar outcome, ...they have a terminal illness, or they've won the lottery, got a new job... or any other of a number of reasons... fact is, they are not there to tell you how they did their job... and it's all too late to get the steps written down by them now.

Here's something else to think about...

You are a prisoner in your own business. When was the last time you got a decent break away from it yet it still continued to operate and make you a profit. Why is that?

It can be said that to do a repetitive task without documenting the process, will mean that you are destined to repeat that task yourself forever if you want it done the same way. The first step in leveraging yourself more time and control, is to step by step record how things should be done, and clearly so that others can do them for you.

Many of you will read that statement and think... how in the world am I going to find time to do all that. Yes, it could be a little bit of a task, but the more important thing to work out first is to ask yourself...

"what is our inefficiency really costing me?"...

If you take the time to think about it, the answer will certainly motivate you into action. If that's not enough, then consider the scenarios I opened this book with and ask yourself...

"what could my lack of systems really cost me?"...

As I explained in the intro, by creating effective systems, things work better and you don't waste time fixing things up or having to re-do work at further expense to your business. Effective systems will save you and your team both time and money.

Highly successful Dentist and author of "The Happiness Centred Business" Paddi Lund tells how he has used systems in his practice to..

"...make difficult things easier to do".

He also says that...

"systems make it possible for us to free our brains while we perform habitual tasks"

 Have you ever tried to do Rubic's Cube? If you are like me, and failed, it was most likely that you were taking a random approach to it. I remember a friend of my daughters teaching her how she follows a simple system to solve Rubic's Cube in a very short space of time.

In effect, once the process has been thought through, and tested, our minds are then free to be more creative, and able to do other things like communicating on a higher level with our clients, whilst performing the routine which has become habit.

"But"... people have said to me... *"my business is different"*.... or... *"there are too many variations of what we do"*. When digging only a little deeper I find that there are a vast number of similarities to other business operations, so I suggest you start somewhere. For example... the basic rule for systemizing your business according to Mike Basch – founder of Federal Express is...

'Systemise the routine, Humanise the exceptions'.

Don't worry about the complicated bits to start with, just focus on the routine stuff which you'll usually find boils down to Pareto's 80:20 rule allowing you to cover the bulk of your work without to many complications.

Anything that cannot be automated using technology needs to be run by people. People-run systems are those repeatable processes and procedures that produce tangible results and quality outcomes for the business.

Always look at putting a system in place rather than employing more people. A system means that things are done consistently, "by-the-numbers", regardless of which team member actually performs the task. Einstein said that...

"Insanity is doing the same thing over and over again, expecting different results".

Happily, from a business owner's perspective,

"Sanity is doing the same thing over and over again, expecting the same or better results".

Why? Consistency and continuous improvement can only be achieved if there is a base to start from. Putting systems in place creates the opportunity for improvement and ultimately provides the only chance to achieve true excellence!

Our clients want consistency...

As the Business Owner you want... the right people, doing the right thing, the right way, and at the right time.

- ✓ *Systems* should run your business consistently and reliably...
- ✓ The right *People* will run your systems and work to improve them...
- ✓ *Your* role is to lead your people to take ownership of their roles...

The well worn comparison is made over and over again...

"Why is it that McDonalds and other successful franchises can all manage to present the same levels of service and quality consistently...with a bunch of teenagers who you can't get to do even the simplest of tasks at home?"

The answer, of course, is that they have well proven systems that everyone is trained to follow... then the youngsters they employ simply turn up at work and follow the system.

While creating systems can seem to be a tedious project to take on... the results show certainly better consistency, and whilst they don't guarantee 100% compliance and your team could divert from following a system, they wouldn't be able to use the old chestnut of an excuse... "I wasn't sure what to do".

.... but where do I start..?

Yes... we need a system to help us build good systems. In the next few chapters you'll learn a couple of simple processes to follow... firstly a process to follow when building new systems, and then another for using when existing systems might not be as effective as you'd like, and therefore need to be reviewed and improved.

Action Steps:
Take a moment now to write in here 3 routine tasks repeated frequently by you in your business that perhaps maybe, perhaps could just be done by someone else.

1. •

2. •

3. •

'Systemise the routine, Humanise the exceptions'.

Chapter 3

How To Build and Improve Systems with LOGIC

We need to break the process down into a few steps and systemisation of a business is mostly a logical process.

There are essentially five basic steps to systemisation when you start documenting your processes and by using "LOGIC" you'll end up with some great systems.

So what is LOGIC, I hear you ask....?

Learn,
Organise,
Generate,
Implement,
Check.

...and it really is all logic in the end.

Learn,

Identify what the processes are that need systemising, and record the way the process is done now. Don't make any changes or variations at this first stage so that you have a record of where you first started.

Organise,

Next we need to organise who, where, what when and why the system will be created.

Generate,

We need then to generate the documentation or systems in a format that can be easily learned from. This can take a multitude of forms, such as manuals, videos, audios, pictures, flowcharts and so on.

Implement,

Put the systems into practice by including all stakeholders and the process and training / educating everyone of how the process should work.

Check.

Measure the outcomes, and get feedback as to the success of the system. For a process of ongoing improvement you can then go to PROFIT.

Let's explore each of these steps in a little more detail, but before we do there are a few hints I'd like to share with you before get into the trenches...

Chapter 4

Hints & Tips to make it all work...

K.I.S.S.. Keep It a Simple System

Firstly, don't over complicate systems or people won't follow them.

Many try to put the whole business process into one system. Break it down into smaller chunks and systemise each chunk.

There is often a "standard" process with a list of potential variables.... a series of what if, or but then... type scenarios, which could also be systemised, or have some rules around how to "humanise" these exceptions.

Make the system for the majority of occasions, and write sub-systems for the variations that may occur.

"A system will work only when it is easier to use the system than ignore it"

Use visual aids

A vast majority of the population learn visually, so use lots of photos, videos, etc. This may be as simple as printing a computer screen or videoing someone doing the task at hand. This will make the systems so much easier to follow.

Make them easy to find and use

Document your system in a policies and procedures or operations manual in an easy to access format.

Make sure everyone knows where to find the systems and processes you develop!

Get Innovative

Someone once said...

> *"Leave it to the laziest person to find the easiest way to do something!".*

While there could be some truth to that statement, systemisation is not meant to encourage laziness, it is meant to promote *innovation*! Always allow and encourage your team to think outside the box and be creative and resourceful.

Unbiased help

It is easier for an outsider to guide the process, especially where businesses want to improve the current status quo, because they don't know "what ought to happen" or "what we always do in this situation," and will document or question everything.

Those with intimate knowledge of the process will be excellent at getting the current scenario in place, but have the tendency to skew the results if reviewing processes. In fact, the single largest challenge for anyone with prior knowledge of the company's processes will be to correct or argue with the results at this stage.

Chapter 5

Learn

Get some quick wins first.

OK, so let's get into the process of creating some systems.

I always like to use systems to improve your profitability, and start off by looking for areas of inefficiency. The results of inefficiency always boil down to 3 key areas, time, cost and quality.

The inevitable result of mismanagement of each of these is lower profits. Identify a level of inefficiency in each case, including time and quality, and you can quickly estimate the hard cost financially to your business through a lack of a good system.

By estimating the cost in hours, or dollars in each of the many areas of business that are typically running inefficiently, you can quickly extrapolate those numbers out to determine what this could be costing you annually. This often includes too many zeros at the end of the number.

The results of these calculations may cause you concern when you realise how big some of these numbers are. However, they could equally cause you great excitement when you realise that by a simple process of systemisation, you could make a huge impact on your time management and profitability.

The doubters among us will want to re-calculate the numbers. Whichever way you look at it, the numbers tell you a story and I urge you to get started somewhere without delay. Procrastination is one of the biggest thieves to your success and it is your choice to stop that happening.

You might be spending too much time micro managing your staff, fixing up errors or re-inventing the wheel each time a task is performed. You might be paying staff for too much un-billable time, managing your stock poorly, or not estimating jobs properly which can all cost unnecessarily. Quality issues may be due to faults getting through to the final stage of production before being identified, warranty re-works, or ineffective training.

These are only a handful of examples and the list is long, each potentially costing your business thousands of dollars which could be added to your profits with the production and following of some simple systems.

Warning...

Some items will undoubtedly jump off the page at you and scream... fix me and you'll be laughing. Sure enough you could generate some big wins fairly quickly and think that's all you need to do, but be warned that *this will be like giving the old girl just another lick of paint...*

You need to address the foundations too and by installing the complete package and systemising the whole business your team will have a different culture ensuring that the benefits are maintained long term.

Look at this as a long term and ongoing project, of constant and never-ending improvement.

Here are a few clues to get you started on some systems that should benefit you immediately...

When figuring out where to start systemising, ask yourself...
- Identify what your hourly rate should be if you were charging a client for your real value.
- Consider what jobs you are doing that you could pay someone a lot less to do for you. Especially identify the jobs that you are doing on a regular basis.
- Are there any jobs which you really don't enjoy doing?
- Pick one to start the ball rolling.

You'll find I'm a fan of checklists, flowcharts and what I call mudmaps (also known as "Mindmaps").

Here is a mind map for part of the Marketing area for a Promotion Products business.

A Mindmap enables you to just throw your thoughts randomly on to paper, or a computer, pulling them into some kind of order as you go, but without getting too bogged down, or distracted by the detail.

Work with your team to develop a mind map for each area or department of your business.

You are charting the path that the work takes through each department.   In some situations it will cross several departments.

When doing this you are working out what your systems will cover. At this stage it does not need to be recorded to the smallest of details... big chunks now, then fill in the gaps later!

A great tool that I have found for doing this is FreeMind which is available for free on-line at www.freemind.sourceforge.net It is an open source application that matches or exceeds the features and capability of most commercial applications.

There are of course other mind mapping applications out there and you can complete this step equally well with any of them. One app that I love on my ipad is iThoughtsHD.

Start by creating a new mind map for your business and create four branches (virtually any business will use these four areas):

- Marketing

- Sales

- Operations – Service or Product Delivery

- Administration/Management

Then work your way through each area showing the functions in that area until such time as the flow of the job is finished or until it passes through to the next area.

Make sure you have listed all the key processes within the area you are working on.

Work with your team and add any missing processes to the area of the mind map you are working on and reword if necessary.

Here is an example of how to expand on the processes:
How the process started:

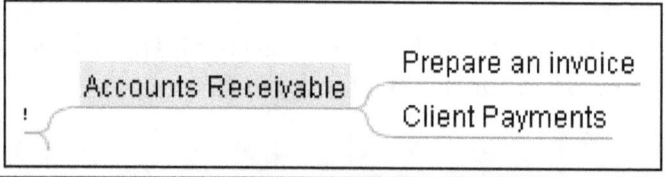

The expanded process:

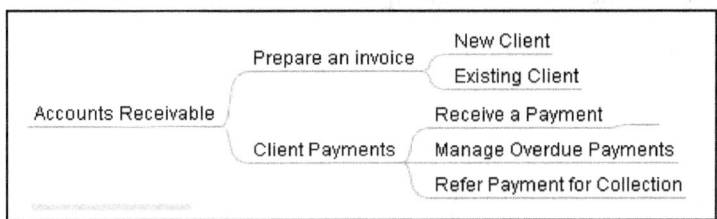

	Prepare an invoice	New Client
		Existing Client
Accounts Receivable		Receive a Payment
	Client Payments	Manage Overdue Payments
		Refer Payment for Collection

Action Steps:
Get yourself a Mind-mapping tool and practice by mapping out the key areas in your business as I have described. Then in each area, highlight the key areas that could provide you some quick wins! Maybe jot them down here until you are in front of a computer.

1. •

2. •

3. •

"A system will work only when it is easier to use the system than ignore it"

Chapter 6

Organise

Begin with the end in mind.

Ok, so that's a bit of an easy statement to make, but there are so many different tasks to "systemise" – how do I know what to work on first.

Of course, as with doing anything properly, you need to plan...

"fail to plan, or plan to fail... your choice!"

You'll need to consider a number of different ways of implementing the systems...

How do you want it to be used in the end, what will it look like, what form should it take, where will the team find it?

Do you need to produce a manual in print, will videos be more useful, or will they be more useful for your team to be on-line or on the company server.

Once you have decided where to start, you'll need a few steps to follow – (would that be a system I hear you asking) – to start to create your first and many other systems.

Identify all tasks

List all the tasks that you can think of that need to be performed in your business.

Clue... don't just do this yourself... enrol your team and get each one of them to list all of their tasks.

Frequency of Task

Note the frequency that these tasks are performed, or should be performed. For example do they happen hourly, daily, weekly, monthly, quarterly, etc.

Rate the Importance

Also, mark against each task the importance of each task to the business. This might be High, Medium, or Low or another scale you choose to make up yourself. Must Do, Should Do, and Could Do is another possibility.

Who is Responsible

Indicate who is responsible for performing this task. Highlight the key stakeholders and who this task affects both upstream and downstream. Who performs tasks immediately prior to this task that might be affected, and who immediately afterwards that will be affected. We need to get feedback and consult with these people to ensure we end up with an efficient and effective system for everyone.

Sign off

Does anyone else need to ensure that this task has been completed. Does an owner or manager need to have sign off.

Will it require a checklist

Mark which tasks require a checklist, or to be part of another checklist to ensure they are done.

Who will create the system

Again... don't try to build all the systems yourself... the best person to develop the system is the person currently doing the job. They are usually much more intimate with the detail and challenges they can experience, so should be more likely than anyone else to get it right.

Identify how well each process of the business currently works

Get a clear picture of how each process of the business currently works including your team in the process, and highlight areas that are not working so well, and /or are critical to your success.

To do this create a key for the mind map making sure you actually put it on the mind map itself so that when you come to look at it a week or so

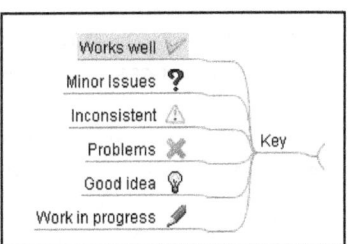

later you know what all the icons mean.

Now work through each area of the business to indicate how well it works. Go with your gut feeling rather than getting into a discussion on each point.

Identify the high value areas of the business. Which parts of the business is it crucial to get right. Where is the money or value created.

Use colours to highlight these areas so that they stand out.

Identify the high value or critical parts of the business that aren't working well. These will be easily identified on the mind map as being the coloured items with a Minor Issues, Inconsistent or Problems icon.

Identify and record the stakeholders for each process on the mind map

This needs to include:
- The Process Owner – this is the person who knows the most about the process – most likely the person doing it

- The Process Team – these are the other team members directly involved with the process

- Team members who work in the process that comes directly before the process/area you're working on

- Team members who work in the process that comes directly after the process you're working on

- Other Stakeholders – those that can contribute to the outcome but have a less direct role in the process. These could also be people upstream or downstream from that process.

You now have a mind map that shows the processes that define your business, and for each of these processes, you'll know who will be involved in mapping the process.

I've thrown a starter checklist in the appendix of this book to give you a few ideas, and I'm sure you'll be able to add to it quite easily.

External Touch Points

Mind-mapping will also give you an idea of how the outside world interacts with your business.

At each 'touch' point you can decide how you want the business to behave whether it's responding to a question or initiating an interaction. Each point raises the need for a string of steps that must be followed to deliver an answer (the "answer" may be a service, delivery of a product or information - whatever it is your business does.)

A hint here. Time is sometimes a trigger that makes the business contact an old client for follow up marketing.

Whilst in many cases you would have a good "gut feeling", this 'modelling' process is a good way of clearly identifying the higher frequency and higher priority functions of the business.

It puts the business in an objective perspective for the business owner.

It gives you an organised way of starting the systemisation of the business.

It gives focus on where you want to be delivering the best service for the best impact with your customers, suppliers, etc.

It gives you the trigger points for the systemisable processes that will occur within the business.
It gives you the processes that you can test and measure.

It allows you to map responsibility for functions against staff roles.

In outline it gives you the whole 'functional architecture' of your business AND because you start prioritising very early in the process, you can focus on adding the highest value in terms of systems and testing or measuring earlier.

Chapter 7

Generate

Break it into Big Chunks...
and then...
Fill in the detailed steps

This is where you get into the detail and start to record your systems. As I mentioned earlier this can be done in many different ways and you'll need to decide what works best for you.

I'll start by asking you to consider whether you think your team would want to read a long descriptive process to learn a system.

Whilst there are occasions where this is important and necessary, typically I find that most would prefer to either watch a video or look at a flowchart for its more visual representation making it a simple thing to follow. Sometimes a simple series of pictures can help paint the picture. Whichever you use, at least you'll be one step ahead of those who do nothing.

Break it into Big Chunks

First thing to make life easy, is to map out the main steps in the process that you might look at as the over simplified system.

Make a Cup of Coffee

For example... if I was writing a system to make a cup of coffee, the simple system might be considered to be...

1. Boil the kettle
2. Put coffee in cup
3. Add boiling water
4. Add milk and sugar

Just by reading these 4 steps you are probably thinking things like, is there water in the kettle, how much coffee, is it instant or ground, or de-caf, how much milk, who said I wanted sugar, etc, highlighting that even for a simple task like this, there are quite a few variables and options that can and will make a difference. So we need to be clear in our instructions.

Fill in the details...

By flowcharting your processes, starting with the big chunks, you'll find it easier to add in all the smaller details, and the options and choices which inevitably lead to the right end result... a bit like when you are doing a jigsaw puzzle and you start off by finding the straight edges and corners first to give you a foundation to build it from.

This will show you how it all fits together.

Document <u>what</u> results are expected, <u>why</u> it is important and <u>how</u> it gets done.

Get the team member who is currently doing the job to record every step required to perform a task.

Once done, give the draft to other stakeholders involved by the system to look for any possible variables that may have been missed, and make the relevant adjustments.

Map the Process – Flowcharting the Steps

Having identified the high value areas of the business start with one of these. Gather together all the stakeholders involved in this process.

Clearly set out the objectives for the session, allocate roles for the session, be clear that everyone is there to actively participate and make sure everyone knows why they have been included in the session.

Be clear on what a successful end result will be for the session. Remember, do not get bogged down on the detail, just get something down and then refine it later.

Consider what does go wrong with the process you are working on at the moment, think about what can go wrong and what is working well.

Warning!! Don't get bogged down with exceptions.

Focus on systemising the routine.... And humanise the exceptions.

You can cover 80% of the eventualities with 20% of the effort, then with the remaining 20% - you'll find you are able to create further systems to cover those, but get the routine sorted first.

Also... Not too dumbed down.

Make it "Cake Box" simple. Write as though the reader does have the ability to do the job comfortably...once they have been shown once. Imagine how instructions on a Cake box are usually down to some basic steps, and they credit the reader with an average level of intelligence. Reserve the detailed explanations for where they are crucial or the process will be too hard to follow when they need to refer back to it for a reminder.

These commonly used figures are standard ISO symbols when creating your flowchart:

The **Terminal** marks the start and finish of the process.

The **Process** shows a single action or step in the process.

The **Decision** allows you to branch the process based on two or more options

The **Document** shows that a form or document is completed at this step.

A **Line** is used to join the figures in the process to show the flow of the process

The **Connector** allows you to skip from one point to another without having to follow a line

As you are mapping the process highlight those steps in the process that need a further detailed written procedure.

Also remember, it is highly likely that changes will be needed at some stage in the future.

Someone might realise that something has been left out or an improvement is discovered. Encourage your team to keep looking for ways to improve the way things are done.

An example of a flowchart showing how to boil an egg is on the next page:

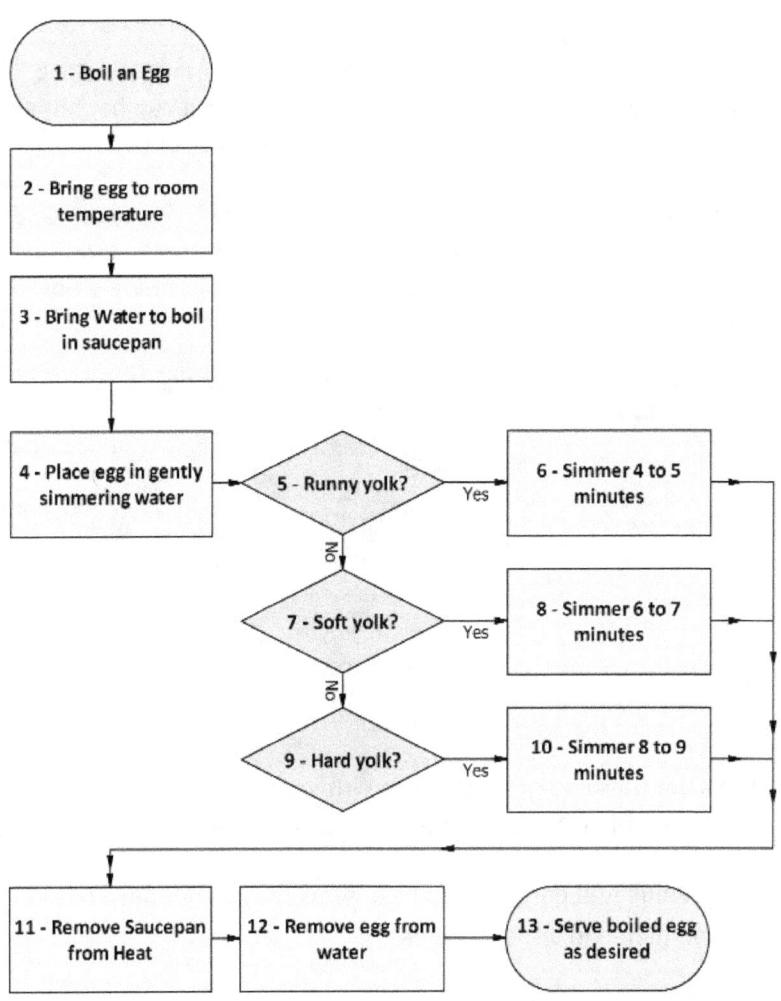

1 - Boil an Egg

2 - Bring egg to room temperature

3 - Bring Water to boil in saucepan

4 - Place egg in gently simmering water

5 - Runny yolk?

Yes → 6 - Simmer 4 to 5 minutes

No

7 - Soft yolk?

Yes → 8 - Simmer 6 to 7 minutes

No

9 - Hard yolk?

Yes → 10 - Simmer 8 to 9 minutes

11 - Remove Saucepan from Heat

12 - Remove egg from water

13 - Serve boiled egg as desired

Add the detail to the Procedure

When producing the procedure apply the KISS Principle – Keep It Simple, Stupid. Ensure you keep it as simple as it can be, but as detailed as it needs to be to get the job done properly.

Use visuals whenever possible and use language and terminology that everyone who needs to can understand and put into practice. Tie the detail here to the appropriate steps in the flow chart.

Consider these points in order to write successful procedures:

• Use numbered paragraphs to show that order is important

• Use bulleted paragraphs to list items that do not need to be completed in a specific order

Example of a Checklist Procedure:

Greeting Telephone Callers Procedure

Mood of telephone calls

Conduct all telephone calls with an atmosphere of:

- Warmth and friendliness
- Patience and good humour
- Interest or enthusiasm

Incoming telephone calls

1. Answer the telephone **within three rings**.
2. Use the words:

   "Welcome to <company name>. <your first name> speaking. How can I help you?"

   a) If the call is for a specific person or role, transfer the call immediately.
   b) If nobody appropriate is available to take the call, record:
      - Caller's name
      - Caller's contact phone number
      - Product/Service they are inquiring about
      - Person or role they want to speak with
      - (If they want to be called back) Suitable time to call back
      - Message or reason for call
      - Time and date of call.
   c) Contact the person called and relay the message.
   d) Deliver the written message to the person called by email and then confirm with a read receipt
   e) If you can't get the message through to the person, ask a fellow team member or manager to follow up the call.

Returning telephone calls

- Return all telephone calls on the same business day or within 24 hours at the latest.
- If you know that you will not be able to return a call in that time, ask another Staff Member to call, apologise and say when you will be available.

By now I guess you are thinking – what do I use to create all this... it sounds like a lot of work.

True... but just think back to the costs of inefficiency that we worked out earlier to give yourself the momentum you need – a job worth doing, is worth doing well... and trust me this is a job worth doing.

But there is an easy way...

I have found a fantastic and very easy to use piece of flowcharting software... with all the flowcharting and documenting built in... plus clever internet based portals and other very handy pieces of software to help you out. I am constantly checking out what is new and effective in the marketplace and I am sure there are others around that offer the tools I have listed above, but I haven't yet found anything more simple to use that has everything I want. If you do, I'd love to hear about them.

For now though... go to my website and check out what I think are the best options available at www.jonesci.com and I have a team as a support arm of my business that will be happy to help you get started. You will find there what I believe to be the complete package for most small business owners (called TKO) at  http://bit.ly/RhMpSk You will find hundreds of pre-drafted documents to modify to your own use in addition to some pretty nifty Project Management tools.

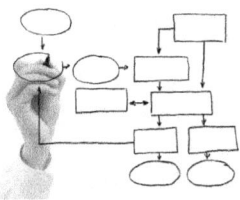

Action Steps:

Have a practice here... draw up a simple flowchart of how you would make a cup of coffee...then ask someone else to follow it.

Chapter 8

Implement

Put the System To Work.

The person putting the process together now needs to do a trial run and get another person to do the task by following the documented steps.

If the person currently doing the task needs to step in and explain anything to the other person then add the missing step etc.

Once completed, if more testing is needed start again with another person until someone can do the task without intervention.

Steps prior to launching the process...

Make sure the process is completely ready with all props ie forms, stamps, checklists etc included.

Consider whether your team will need any training with the introduction of the process, and if needed who will do it.

Decide who will introduce the process to your team, when and what the best way to do this is.

Decide how you will handle feedback on the process. Some ways include by survey, discussions or interviews.

Sign Off on the Process
This might be verbal or involve signing and filing a copy of the process involving all responsible parties. Be consistent with what you do, then set up a review cycle.

Change Management techniques...

Implementation can often involve requiring some change and this needs to be handled correctly. Much has been written about change management, but it's worth giving a quick mention here to the widely used "**RACI**" method.

RACI stands for Responsible, Accountable, Contribute, and Informed.

Responsible is the "doer" – whoever it is that has been made responsible for completion of the task.

Accountable is the person with their backside on the line. Someone who the responsibility might ultimately lie with, but may not necessarily be doing the job.

Contribute can also be "**Consult**" and is the other parties involved who can help along the process of change, and may have valuable input to offer. This might be for example those up or down line of the process being systemised.

Informed is effectively just that, making sure that everyone is informed of the change.

Recognising everyone affected and involved in any change is important to ensuring that any change is not undone by failing to involve or inform the relevant people. Imagine thrusting a new system on to someone who wasn't involved who then potentially feels unworthy or dis-interested... are they going to go out of their way to make it work?

This is probably a good time to look at potential roadblocks that you might need to be prepared for.

11 Potential Obstacles to Consider

There are several potential pitfalls to implementing systems into a business. Many of these are inter-related so let's have a look at them now...

1. Resistance
Resistance can come from fear... not knowing why or how, and generally brought about by lack of or poor communication.

2. Nobody owning the process

As is often the case in any area of endeavour... if no-one is responsible, then it is left to chance whether or not something is achieved. If implementation and monitoring is made the responsibility of someone then there is ownership and accountability to follow through.

3. People feeling excluded

Don't just pick one person in the team to help develop a system without the inclusion of the others. Certainly you can have one person work on it initially, but it is important that the rest of the team is informed that the process will be discussed with them for their inclusion and feedback, but for economical reasons you don't want everyone on the team spending time on the whole process.

4. High expectations from management with low support

Team members are usually willing to help develop the business and systems especially where the management takes the time to support that team member. Don't just leave them to it without giving them the resources or time required to complete it properly.

5. Loss of Momentum

Many a great opportunity is lost to us, through the daily demands of business. Often this is due to lack of one thing... prioritising in a weekly plan. Whilst in the initial phase people will generate their own momentum, after time passes other things take precedence and momentum is lost. However, with some goals, a plan, tracking, and recognition can be maintained. Another challenge is being too ambitious with the goals in the beginning and then not achieving them, so this can slow momentum even more.

6. Management Sabotaging the system

If management takes short-cuts, it sends the message to everyone else that the system is not that important, so instantly diminishes the value of having a system at all... This could affect not only that particular process, but other systems too could be affected by this mindset, so everyone needs to follow it.

7. Lack of tracking or Celebration

Catch people doing the right thing. When was the last time you got up in the morning and set out to do something wrong at work? Probably never if you are like 99% of the population... people try to do the right thing, and they like to hear they are doing the right thing. So often though, they only hear when they have done the wrong thing... so get negative feedback. Remember that positive reinforcement produces positive results.

8. Poor Communication

If something goes wrong, look first to the system for the problem and not the person. More often than not roles and systems to follow are either poorly introduced or simply "abdicated". By following a proper process to train and implement changes or new systems the likelihood of the team being able to do things correctly will increase.

9. Personality Styles

Probably a totally separate subject to cover, but it is important to recognise that as humans we all have different styles. Some just love following systems and the detail, whilst the more creative and impulsive among us like the freedom to do as they will. Our systems need to recognise this and be kept simple enough to follow without being restrictive.

10. Learning Styles
Remember to use the most appropriate medium to show the system, such as using audio, video, pictures, charts, and diagrams to cover everyone's different learning styles.

11. Systems not being kept up to date.
Fairly simply... if you make a change to the process, then update the system. Also, make sure that there is only one version of the system, so that everyone is working on the same page. Version tracking should be used as a safeguard so that everyone knows they have the current issue.

Action Steps:
Take a few moments to list out any potential roadblocks that you need to address.

1. •

2. •

3. •

4. •

5. •

6. •

7. •

Chapter 9

Check

Time to test it out.

Remember, now that your system is implemented, you need to keep it live and up to date. First thing to do is to test and monitor it.

Working closely with them, have someone follow the procedure to test it out. Often this can be best tested using someone unfamiliar with the task as they would have less opportunity to second guess the procedure written down, and have to follow it more precisely.

Set Up a Review Cycle

When setting up your review cycle timeline consider these factors...

- How familiar are your team members with the requirements of this process?
- List all the points you will need to discuss when you launch the process.

- Do your team members need to learn any new skills or ways of doing things?
- How would you rate the level of risk in the process (Low, Medium or High)... as well as physical risks such as damage or injury. Consider other risks such as to your business image or the environment.

Based on your answers set in place a time to review the process either as at a certain date or after a number of cycles to see if this process is performing and producing as you intend it to.

Test and measure performance to find out how your systems are really helping your business and survey clients to find out where your systems might be letting you down.

Measure results using key performance indicators (KPIs). Generally, there will be measures to show system performance. You can often find these from the person doing the job, but often it can be following processes that can pick up where things aren't working so well.

For example in sales you could measure the number of leads, conversion rate, average $ sale etc to measure each stage of the sales process. In a production operation it might be the next stage of production that measures the success rate of the previous stage to highlight how production stages are performing.

Allow and encourage the system to change/grow.

Encourage your team to continuously look for ways to improve processes and to give you feedback and reward them when they find and fix errors.

There are a number of ways to make this happen...
1. Incorporate system references in staff compensation plans.
2. Reward high performance.
3. Reward employees for suggestions to enhance the systems.
4. Ensure that the systems are self-correcting and can evolve.

Don't let the rot set in

Having opened the opportunity for improvements to be made, these should not just be allowed ad-hoc.

If you allow someone to stray from the system today, they will again tomorrow, and by next week it will be routine.

Everyone needs to follow the system, regardless of what position or status they are in the business. By allowing someone who *"has always done it a different way"* or the boss to take a short-cut, sends a strong message to the rest of the team that it is OK to not follow the system... then the rot sets in.

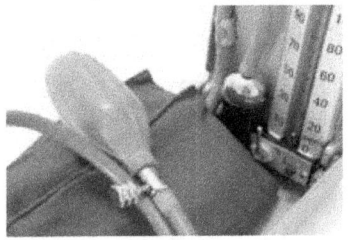

Chapter 10

You Can Profit If It Doesn't Work.

How to fix up the systems that don't work so well.

Undoubtedly, you will periodically identify systems that aren't working so well, or you find problems have occurred that need review. Where these things occur, to improve your systems you need to follow a slightly modified process...

I call this the **PROFIT** process and it flows similar to LOGIC but with some simple variations...

Problem,

Review,

Options,

Fine-tune,

Implement,

Test.

PROFIT is not dis-similar to LOGIC so the main detail can be taken from previous chapters. You'll find though that PROFIT will keep you focussed on the "improvement" process rather than the "creation" process.

Problem,

Firstly identify and accept that there is a problem with something in your business not working as effectively or efficiently... if at all... Highlight it as a "Problem" that needs addressing.

Review,

Analyse the problem and assess it's implications, as well as the priority level it requires to be rectified.

Options,

Next we need to consult the relevant people involved with this issue, directly and indirectly, explore the options for improvements that are available for us, and record them to help us make the relevant decisions later.

Fine-tune,

Pick what appears to be the best option and then fine-tune all steps required to address the issue, and document them clearly.

Implement,

Put the systems into practice by including all stakeholders and the process and training / educating everyone of how the process should work.

Test.

Measure the outcomes, and get feedback as to the success of the system. For a continued process of ongoing improvement you can then go back to the beginning of PROFIT and repeat the cycle as a process of constant improvement.

Chapter 11

Set Some Goals

At the time when the business started the originator, possibly you, would have had a set of expectations, processes, and priorities in mind possibly derived from when they originally did all the work themselves.

This step should pull out those expectations, the priorities for the company, and the priorities for the owner. For example, the owner thinks that a thank you is being sent after every payment received, but the processes of "Systemology" shows that they are only being sent when past dues payments are received. This gives opportunity to correct that and make the business operation more consistent in the long term.

The "Systemology" of a whole business can and probably will take some time, so rather the trying to do the whole thing at once, you'll need to set some goals.

How to set some goals

You want this process to focus on two things: What's best for the owner and what's most cost effective for the business.

You'll want complete participation and buy in from the team on the final product. The key stakeholders need to meet and set the priorities and set some goals. A widely accepted rule to follow to gauge whether or not your goals are well written is to follow the process of writing S.M.A.R.T (Specific, Measurable, Achievable, Results Focussed, and Time-framed) goals. If your goals don't meet each of these criteria then they need more attention to ensure they are goals that can work for you.

It is advisable to choose to include team members in setting these goals as well. Your strategic management can't dictate what is right from the top if there is significant divergence here (and there frequently is in medium sized businesses where the owner or management is less involved in day-to-day operations).

You will want any training in the future to be in line with the systems created.

This will require that everyone has a clear and positive understanding throughout the organization that the systems manuals are dynamic and living – "this is how we do it now, but if the business changes or if someone comes up with a better way, we will change".

The whole company needs to come away with a commitment and a plan for continuous self-audit using KPIs and then "PROFIT" to make sure that the business is operating the way it should optimally and to evaluate and incorporate any innovations that surface in the future.

Chapter 12

Where should we start...

We now know the "system" to follow to create our systems and start working towards that dream of independency from your business... or at least of making it work for you.

Let's now explore what processes there are that we can document to make everyone's lives better.

As you read through the checklist in this chapter you will start to realize (if you haven't already) how successful business people have drilled down into every area of their businesses and worked with their team to create systems in just about every aspect of the business.

The checklist highlights the majority of areas that most businesses will be able to take control of by producing and working to a set process or system...

It's about then that you might start to feel a little overwhelmed by the task ahead, however you'll find though that in many of these areas your team will be quite quickly be able to pull together some draft systems following the **LOGIC** process as they are already doing them repeatedly.

You will then focus on the mission critical processes in your business, and problem areas, and improve them with **PROFIT**.

Here's your starter list...

Daily Office Operation Systems
- Answering the telephone
- Receiving and opening the mail
- Purchasing and maintaining office supplies and equipment
- Faxing and e-mailing
- Dealing with incoming/outgoing delivery needs
- Backing up and archiving data

Product Development Systems
- Developing product and protecting it legally
- Developing packaging and collateral material (eg catalogues)
- Developing manufacturing methods and process
- Developing manufacturing costing and bidding process

Manufacturing And Inventory Systems
- Selecting vendors
- Determining product or service warranties offered
- Establish product or service pricing (retail and wholesale)
- Establishing reorder process for inventory production

- Receiving and storing product as inventory
- Reconciling physical inventory with accounting records

Order Processing And Tracking Systems
- Taking orders and recording the orders by mail, fax, phone or online
- Fulfilling and packaging the orders
- Confirming details before service or product delivery
- Sending/Shipping the orders
- Management system for freight, couriers and vehicles
- Order tracking systems

Invoicing and Accounts Receivable Systems
- Invoicing customers for the orders
- Receiving payments for the orders and crediting customers for payment (whether cash, check or credit card)
- Monitoring credit control and age of accounts
- Management of the collection process for outstanding receivables

Customer Service Systems
- Returns procedure for inventory receiving and customer payment return
- Responding to customer complaints/inquiries
- Replacing defective product or performing other warranty service
- Measure quality and professionalism of service delivery
- Referral Management System

- Acquiring Testimonials

Accounts Payable Systems
- Purchasing procedures and approvals required
- Payment process for supplies and inventory
- Petty cash

Sales and Marketing Systems
- Create an overall marketing plan
- Sales Process/Scripting
- Designing and producing promotional materials
- Developing general leads and prospects
- Creating an advertising plan
- Creating a public relations plan
- Creating a direct mail plan
- Developing and maintaining a database
- Developing and maintaining a website
- Analysing and tracking sales statistics
  - Continuously measure number and origin of all leads
  - Measure conversion rate for each salesperson
  - Measure your average dollar sale for every team member
  - Keep a record of your profit margins
- Contract Terms and Conditions
- Contract Approval and Booking Procedures

People and Education Systems
- Time management
- Meeting management
- Recruitment procedures

- Training employees
- Working out Personality and Learning Styles
- Payroll process/Compensation Plans
- Employee Orientation/Induction program
- Organisation chart
- Team member positional contracts/Job Descriptions
- Career planning
- Company rules of the game/Code of Ethics
- Company vision and mission statement
- Company and individual team member goals and performance indicators
- Belief and Identity growth processes
- Conflict resolution
- Contingency staffing plans
- Redundancy systems

General Accounting Systems
- Managing the accounting process with daily, weekly, monthly, quarterly and annual reports
  - Complete and keep to monthly and yearly budgets
  - Complete a monthly balance sheet
  - Daily or weekly update cash-flow statements
- Managing cash with future borrowing needs secured and available
- Budgeting and forecasting
- Reporting payroll taxes, superannuation and withholding payments
- Complete weekly bank reconciliation
- Have a daily banking system
- Maintaining an asset register including depreciation

General Corporate Systems
- Negotiating, drafting and executing contracts
- Developing and protecting intellectual property
- Managing insurance needs and coverage
- Reporting and paying federal, state and other taxes
- Planning for federal, state and other taxes
- Managing and storing records
- Maintenance of equipment
- Maintaining investor/shareholder relations
- Information flow processes
- Ensuring legal security
- Developing a business plan for planning and managing growth

Physical Space Management Systems
- Maintaining and designing telephone and electrical systems
- Upgrading office equipment
- Planning permits and fees
- Licensing
- Ensuring physical security

...and finally... a System to control your Systems and ensure they are kept alive and current.

Chapter 13

Conclusion

Why do I talk about "turbo-charging business systematically"?

I hope that you have found some inspiration in this book to get you motivated towards building some systems in your business. This might not be the most glamorous side of running a business, but it is the engine room.

I don't make the relationship to turbo-charged engines without reason. Many of us don't have a big V8 business... but could quite easily turbo-charge what we do have.

You've probably heard the word "turbo" tossed around a lot, especially by performance car enthusiasts. But all most of us know is that it means an engine has more "oomph" to it than normal. To give your business more "oomph"... look at turbo-charging it....systematically!

Internal combustion engines are "breathing" engines. That is to say, they draw in air and fuel for energy. This energy is realized as power when the air-fuel mixture is ignited. Afterwards, the waste created by the combustion is expelled as exhaust gases. This is your average business... not bad, but could do better!

A turbocharger makes the air-fuel mixture more combustible by fitting more air into the engine's chambers which creates more power and torque when the piston is forced downward by the resulting explosion. It does this by compressing, the air molecules so that the air the engine draws in is denser. So how can you do this with your business...?

Think about how you can squeeze more energy out of what it currently has... where are you currently wasting energy?

A turbocharger is basically an air pump. Hot exhaust gases leaving the engine after combustion are routed directly to the turbine wheel side of the turbocharger to make it rotate. That turbine wheel is connected to a compressor wheel. As the turbine wheel spins faster and faster, so then the compressor wheel must also spin quickly. The rotation of the compressor wheel pulls in air and compresses it before pumping it into the engine's chambers giving more power.

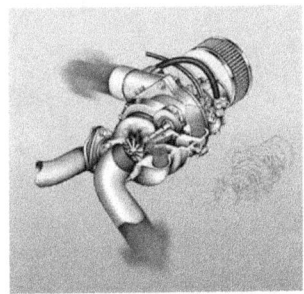
The basic principal behind turbo-charging is fairly simple, but a turbocharger is a very complex piece of machinery. Not only must the components within the turbocharger itself be precisely coordinated, but the turbocharger and the engine it services must also be exactly matched. If they're not, engine inefficiency and even damage can be the result. That's why it's important to follow correct installation, operating and preventative maintenance procedures.

In concluding, make this comparison to your business now, using similar wording... The basic principal behind business is fairly simple, but a business is a very complex piece of machinery. Not only must the components within the business itself be precisely coordinated, but the business and the owners it services must also be exactly matched. If they're not, owner inefficiency and even damage can be the results. That's why it's important to follow correct installation, operating and preventative maintenance procedures... take the time and put the right systems into your business so that it can serve you with more "oomph" and not break down because you haven't put it together properly.

Remember...System stands for "Saving Your Self Time Energy & Money"...

Credit where it's due...

As I mentioned early in the book, I don't profess to be the creator of all these great ideas, merely the person who has learned from many others, used and tested their ideas, and pulled together what I intend to be a book of useful reference for those wanting a better life through a business that can work independently of them being hands on at all times.

I want therefore to acknowledge those that have helped me in my learning and recognise that some of the ideas in this book have been taught to me be them, or adapted from things very similar.

Bradley J Sugars – CEO and Founder of ActionCOACH Business Coaching... my mentor in recent years, from whom I have taken a great deal of inspiration, education and motivation. Brad is an inspiration to many and has certainly changed the way I approach a number of things in business and life in general.

John Tonkin – Brain in a Box... Quite a guru in the field of building business systems, and the creator of the magic tool "Brain In A Box".

Adrian Payne – The Village Scribe for his support and creativity in helping me bring this book to print.... and an awesome front cover.

Kerrie Hourigan, Kylee Legge and Rochelle Stone – For their separate guidance in how to publish and the initial marketing of this book.

The Business Systems 360 Review.

Guaranteed to find you at least 20 x your investment.

We don't know what we don't know! We all know we should regularly go to a doctor for a thorough check-up, and we're better off finding out before it's too late if something needs attention.... But when was the last time you took time out to review how well your business was functioning? This is often thought about at the time of a major milestone or decision to be made... but why wait until then when you could benefit now?

Raise The Bar!

You are probably familiar with the term "Comfort Zones"... Just as the best in sport have their specialists to help them lift their game, business owners also need someone to help them lift theirs. Even the most successful businesses are haemorrhaging profits, some more than others, and through a wide range of potential inefficiencies, so our goal is to prevent that as much as we can. As humans we get comfortable with what we are doing daily, and often miss those improvements by not stepping out and challenging occasionally, the comfort zones that we immerse ourselves in.

> "We have found about $100,000 through this review... It certainly was beneficial to have 'outside eyes' looking at my business and helping to point me in the right direction..."Graham

Tell-tale Signs Of Inefficiency

Businesses can experience or be at risk of diseconomies of scale through growth by acquisition of other businesses, booms in organic growth (new partner or investor or bank loan), adopting more products/services/market areas, or the securing of a major tender/supplier, loss of valuable management resources at the wrong time...and quite simply.. ineffective or poor systems and processes to drive their business. Tell-tale signs that companies experience when these things occur include...

- Being late on delivery deadlines, and slow to react to client demands, or competitive threats.
- A rising cost of sale.
- Falling workforce morale including Management Stress through, Absenteeism, Decent or Fighting/conflict.
- Growth has stalled
- High levels of waste.
- Increasing debt

Is It For Me?
If you haven't analysed your business properly for a long time, if ever... now is _always_ a great time. However, **it's vital if you are experiencing any challenges already mentioned or are considering...**

- ...purchasing other companies.
- ...adding to the management team, or sales team....or taking on new partners,
- ...looking at investment loans or expansions to an overdraft,
- ...winning a large tender, or the distribution rights of a significant product or service
- ...consolidation from a Cash-flow management focus, or Work force and/or Supplier rationalisation.
- ...readying your business or business system for sale by franchising, or opening more branches
- ...or simply to maximise your returns in your exit strategy and succession planning
  "It will help your business immensely"- **Scott**

How does it work?
We start with a series of questions and checklists to run through to review you and your business. Casting a systematic magnifying glass over the whole business to explore all avenues of opportunity for you to build upon, we will examine how well you have systemised...

- your goal setting and planning to take you to them,
- your financial management and your understanding of what it all means,
- the consistency of delivery of your goods or services,
- how you manage your time and yourself,
- everything to do with marketing your niche
- and then how you convert this marketing into sales,
- your documentation and systemisation including the technology you use,
- and of course, your team, leadership and the complications that all that can involve.
- We also offer the option of independent supplier and customer surveys to gain their perspective on your business too.

You'll get some great ideas...
As part of this process you'll want to have a notepad handy as in the simple process of our asking some of these probing questions, you'll have some "Blinding Flashes of the Obvious" ... those little pots of gold that you'll want to rush away and implement straight away... but that's normal, let's just start by capturing them and then we'll help you pull them all together into your plan when the timing is right.

Is it complicated?
No, most of what we work on is not rocket science and you'll be able to answer most of the questions off the top of your head, though some may take a bit of research and highlight some areas that need to be worked on to bring into the business. Be prepared for some challenging questions too, but you'd expect that to grow you need to take on some challenges.

What is the Outcome?
We compile an easy to understand report for you to keep and digest for implementing in your business. You'll also be given some options for your next steps to take to get some quick gains and solve some challenges. Our philosophy is to be there for you for the long haul... not

just a quick fix... or even just a lot of promises. We will identify a number of things that can be done to make you and your business more effective and efficient... but we don't leave you all excited and not knowing what to do next. The key thing is, that if we identify some decent opportunities for you... then our goal is to make sure you can capitalise on them, regardless of how much you want us to be involved.

20 x Guarantee

If the process of the Business Systems 360 fails to identify the potential for at least 20 times the value of your investment, we will refund the entire investment in full, and still deliver your report at no further cost..!!

Contact Clive and his Team
for support and any of the software mentioned in this book.

- **Speaking Engagements and Workshops**

- **Turbocharged Business Tips & Book Reviews in the Vault at**
  www.clivejones.com.au

- **Coaching – ActionCOACH Business & Executive Coaching**
  The Worlds #1 Business Coaching Firm.
  www.actioncoach.com/clivejones

- **Systems Consulting Team - Jonesci**
  www.jonesci.com

www.ingramcontent.com/pod-product-compliance
Lightning Source LLC
Chambersburg PA
CBHW071243170526
45165CB00003B/1224